FOR JACK
M. M.

FOR FRANCESCA DOW
J. R.

Text copyright © 1996 by Margaret Mayo

Illustrations copyright © 1996 by Jane Ray

All rights reserved.

CIP Data is available.

First published in the United States 1997 by

Dutton Children's Books, a division of Penguin Books USA Inc.

375 Hudson Street, New York, New York 10014

Originally published in Great Britain 1996 by Orchard Books, London

Printed in Singapore

FIRST AMERICAN EDITION

1 3 5 7 9 10 8 6 4 2

ISBN 0-525-45788-7

MYTHICAL BIRDS & BEASTS

FROM MANY LANDS

MYTHICAL
Birds & Beasts
FROM MANY LANDS

retold by MARGARET MAYO

illustrated by Jane Ray

DUTTON CHILDREN'S BOOKS

NEW YORK

⋄ Contents ⋄

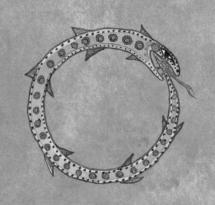

Pegasus: The Chimera

THE HORSE THAT COULD FLY

Pegasus was a beautiful, wild, snow-white horse with huge feathered wings that allowed him to fly. In the far-off times when gods lived on earth, Pegasus freely roamed the land of Greece. No one had ever ridden him. No one had ever gotten close enough to touch him—until a certain young prince learned the secret of taming this wonderful flying horse.

The prince's name was Bellerophon. He was a handsome, lively, and daring prince who loved travel and adventure. But he was not perfect. Who is? Prince Bellerophon's trouble was that he thought too much of himself and believed he could do anything. Actually, he was something of a show-off!

On his travels the prince heard about King Iobates, who ruled a country called Lycia, to the north of Greece. King Iobates was rich, *and* he had a lovely daughter, *and* he had promised she would marry anyone who could kill a truly awful, ferocious, three-headed monster that was rampaging around the country, breathing out fire and destroying everything.

"I shall go to Lycia," Prince Bellerophon thought to himself, "straightaway." And he did.

When the prince arrived, he was welcomed by King Iobates and invited to a feast where everyone was talking about the three-headed monster and nothing else. The monster was called the Chimera, and she really was weird-looking. She had a lion's head at the front of her body and a goat's head growing out of her middle. Where her tail should have been was a long, twisty snake instead. The Chimera had lion's legs and claws but the shaggy body of a goat. Most frightening of all, from each of her three mouths she blasted out fierce flames and vile-smelling poisonous fumes.

"Wherever she goes, she burns and destroys," said the king. "My bravest heroes have gone out to hunt her, but not one has returned. It's impossible to kill the Chimera!"

"There must be a way...." murmured Bellerophon, almost to himself. "It must be possible."

The king was annoyed. "So you, my fine prince, are going to rid us of the monster! Good! Come back when you've done it!"

And Bellerophon, who was such a proud young man, looked straight at the king and said, "I shall try!"

That night Bellerophon lay awake, trying to work out how he could kill the Chimera. "If only I could shoot at her with arrows from above," he thought. "From just beyond the reach of her fierce flames and deadly breath. If only I could fly...." And then he remembered Pegasus. "I must find the winged horse—catch him and tame him."

Now, Bellerophon, like everyone else, believed that the winged horse belonged to the gods. So he took his bow and arrows, boarded a ship, and sailed to Greece. When he arrived, he went to the temple of the goddess Athena and prayed for her help.

The prince was tired, so he lay down while he waited for a message from the goddess. Just before dawn he fell asleep. He dreamed that a slender woman, dressed in white, stood beside him. In her hands she held a horse's bridle made of gold. "Take this," she said. "With it you can tame Pegasus. He can be found by an enchanted pool, which he made with one stamp of his hoof. The pool is high up on the mountain called Helicon."

When the prince woke, he saw a golden horse's bridle lying on the floor beside him. He picked it up and examined it carefully. Then, with his bow across his shoulder and the bridle in his hand, he set off to find the enchanted pool.

He walked and walked until he came to the mountain called Helicon. He climbed its slopes and at last found a place where cool, clear water bubbled up into a pool shaped like a large horse's hoof.

Bellerophon sat down a little way off, resting his back against the trunk of a gnarled old olive tree. He waited, but Pegasus didn't come. When it grew dark, the prince fell asleep.

In the morning he was awakened by the sound of great wings beating steadily. He looked up, and it seemed to him as if an enormous snow-white bird with glistening, silver-tipped wings was flying toward the mountain. But this was not a bird. It was Pegasus.

The wingbeats grew slower, and the wonderful horse came gliding down and landed beside the pool. Folding his wings, he lowered his beautiful snow-white head and began to drink.

Slowly the prince rose to his feet. Slowly he took the bridle in his hands and tiptoed toward Pegasus. The horse looked up, snorted loudly, and stamped his hooves. He spread his wings, ready to fly. But then he caught sight of the golden bridle. Immediately Pegasus folded his wings and waited, quiet as a lamb, until the prince came right up beside him and slipped the golden bit into his mouth.

The prince stroked the horse's long white mane and gently touched the silver-tipped wings. "Pegasus, greatest of horses," he said. "Take me to Lycia and help me kill that terrible monster the Chimera!"

The prince laid both his hands between the folded wings, jumped lightly onto the horse's back, and took hold of the golden reins. "Now fly!" he called out. Pegasus spread his wings, slowly beat them up and down, and leaped into the air.

Up and up they soared together, Pegasus flying faster and faster. How Prince Bellerophon enjoyed himself, riding high in the sky and looking down at the world below! "This," he said, "is the best and only way to travel!"

They flew on, and in a few hours they reached Lycia. At first the countryside below was full of color and alive with people and animals. There were fruit trees and vines growing on the hillsides, bright vegetable patches, wildflowers, and fields of corn. But before long they came to a place that had been utterly destroyed by fire. The grass, the trees, every single plant was blackened. The houses were empty, burnt-out ruins. There were no men or women, no children or animals. Everything was dead.

Still they flew on, looking for the Chimera, until Bellerophon saw smoke drifting out from the mouth of a cave. "That cave must be the Chimera's den," he said to Pegasus. "Fly down. Let's have a closer look."

Down swooped Pegasus, neighing loudly. The Chimera heard. She gave a long, loud lion's roar and came padding out

of her cave. When she saw Pegasus and the prince, she leaped toward them, long, fierce flames and poisonous fumes spouting from her three mouths. The heat was almost unbearable, and the smell of the fumes was vile.

But Prince Bellerophon let go of the golden reins and, gripping the horse with his knees, fixed an arrow in his bow. He took aim and fired, and the arrow struck the Chimera in her lion's throat. The monster roared and belched out more flames and fumes, so thick the prince could hardly breathe. That would have been the end of him, except the wonderful horse swiftly swerved sideways and flew upward until they reached cool fresh air again.

When they had both recovered, the prince urged Pegasus to dive down once more into the smoke and flames. The prince took aim again, and this time his arrow pierced the monster's heart. The Chimera stumbled and fell to the ground, writhing and rolling around, roaring loudly in her pain and fury.

Then horse and rider rose up again and hovered in the cool fresh air, waiting. After a while the flames died down, the smoke began to clear, and they could see that the monster lay on the ground, quiet and still. The Chimera was dead.

The prince patted Pegasus fondly on the neck. "Wonderful horse," he said, "our work is done, so take me now to King Iobates's palace." With a shake of the golden reins, they were off, flying through the air.

When the prince arrived at the palace with Pegasus and told the king that they had killed the Chimera, there were, as

you can imagine, many smiles and lots of congratulations all around. A big celebration feast was held, because everyone was relieved that the terrible Chimera was dead and that the country had been saved from further destruction.

And then? Not long after, the handsome prince married the king's only daughter *and* became heir to the kingdom! And of course he still had the golden bridle, so he often rode the wonderful horse Pegasus. Prince Bellerophon was happy.

And that should have been the end of the story. But remember, the prince had thought rather a lot of himself to begin with and believed he could do anything. Well, as time went by, he became an even *bigger* show-off! He would say, "Who killed the Chimera? I did! Has anyone else a horse like mine? *No one!* I am...*just like the gods!*"

He couldn't stop thinking how amazingly clever and important he was, until one day he decided to visit the gods

in their earthly home on Mount Olympus. So he placed the golden bridle on Pegasus and told him to fly to Olympus.

Pegasus rose up into the air, higher and higher. He set his head toward Mount Olympus and flew.

But the gods see everything. And Zeus, king of the gods, was angry. "So this proud young man thinks he is just like a god!" Zeus exclaimed.

He sent out an insect with a very sharp sting. When it stung Pegasus, the wonderful horse was so surprised that he reared up and threw Prince Bellerophon off his back. The prince fell down, down, all the way to the ground—and he died.

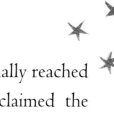

But Pegasus continued his journey. When he finally reached Olympus, the gods welcomed him, and Zeus claimed the horse for his own special use.

"Pegasus," he said, "whenever I make storms in the sky, you shall carry the thunder and lightning bolts for me."

And to this day, Pegasus works for Zeus. So, next time the thunder rolls and lightning flashes, look up. If you are lucky, you may catch a glimpse of Pegasus, the winged horse, charging across the sky.

A Greek myth

The Mermaid

DON'T EVER LOOK AT A MERMAID

Once there was a young fisherman called Lutey, who one day met a mermaid face-to-face. Now, that's a rare thing to happen to anyone. And it's rarer still to meet a mermaid and live to tell about it. But Lutey did.

Lutey lived in a cottage overlooking the sea, together with his wife, three lively sons, and a large, brown, lolloping, and most affectionate dog named Towser. And it just so happened that one morning Lutey went for a stroll on the beach, with Towser lolloping at his heels.

The tide was out, and the rippled sands were still wet. The waves were lap-lap-lapping as they rolled ashore. Then, all of a sudden, Lutey heard a strange, mournful cry: *"Aaa-ooooo!"* The sound came from behind a pile of rocks that jutted out onto the shore. What could it be?

He hurried forward. Behind the rocks was a shallow pool, fringed by more rocks and separated from the sea by a wide stretch of sand. Lutey gasped. He couldn't believe what he saw. There, on one of the rocks, sat a mermaid. She was the most beautiful creature he had ever seen. Her skin was as white and smooth as marble. Her hair was long and golden. And she had a wonderful, curving, greenish-blue tail that shimmered softly in the morning sun.

As soon as she saw him, she called out, "Have pity, good man, and help me."

Lutey knew that mermaids were unlucky creatures. He knew the fishermen's saying: "Don't ever look at a mermaid!" But she was so beautiful he couldn't take his eyes off her.

"My name is Lutey," he said, "but who are you? And how can I help you?"

"I am Morvena," she answered. "And I've been sitting here so busy combing my hair and gazing at myself in the water that I didn't notice the tide go out. Now I can't get back to the sea unless…unless, Lutey, you carry me across the sands. If you do, I'll pay you well."

Lutey laughed. "What can you possibly give to me?"

"I can give you three wishes," she answered.

"Three wishes! Oh! I know what I want. I've often thought about it!" exclaimed Lutey. "Not money. No. Nothing like that."

"Think carefully," said the mermaid. "Very carefully. Then choose what you want."

"What I would like," said Lutey quietly, "is the power to heal people when they're sick, the power to make them well and strong again."

"A healer. The gift is yours," she said. "And what else?"

"I would like," he said, "the power to break wicked spells that make folk so angry they end up quarreling and hurting one another."

"A peacemaker. The gift is yours. And one more?"

"I would like these powers to continue after I die," said Lutey. "I would like them to pass down through my family, forever."

"The gift is yours," said the mermaid. "So now carry me to the sea."

She reached out her white arms and wrapped them around Lutey's neck. But as he lifted her, Towser began to whine. It was a long, low, eerie whine.

Lutey became afraid. "How can I know you won't harm me?" he asked.

Morvena touched her hair and took out a golden comb, all

delicately patterned and set with tiny pearls. "Take this as a token," she said. Then she smiled at him, and Lutey forgot his fear.

"That's a real beauty!" he said as he slipped the golden comb into his trouser pocket, where he kept various odds and ends—some string, a pocketknife, and so on.

Then Morvena began to sing. She sang about secret caves and enchanted palaces under the sea. She sang about a life free from pain, death, and sadness. As though in a dream, Lutey began to walk across the sands, his dog, Towser, following and whining. But Lutey had ears only for the mermaid's songs.

Lutey reached the sea and waded in. But now Towser didn't follow. He stayed at the water's edge, still whining.

Lutey waded on, and when the water came to the top of his legs, he said to the mermaid, "Now you can swim off."

"Deeper, deeper," sang Morvena. "Take me deeper."

Lutey waded out farther until the water reached his waist. "Now swim off," he said.

But Morvena only sang, "Deeper, deeper…take me deeper."

Lutey waded out until the water reached his shoulders. "I can go no farther," he said, trying to lower her into the water. But she wrapped her arms more tightly around his neck and wound her tail about his legs.

"Come, come…come with me," she sang in his ear. She sang and sang, until the only thing Lutey wanted was to go with her.

And then Towser barked. Again and again he barked, loud and fierce, until the shore echoed with his barking. At last Lutey heard him and looked back. He saw his large, brown, lolloping, and most affectionate dog by the water's edge. Lutey looked beyond and saw his three lively sons and his own dear wife standing by the cottage door.

"Let me go!" he cried. "I cannot leave my family to come with you!"

But Morvena only tightened her grasp and tried to pull Lutey's head down into the water. Lutey struggled, but though the mermaid was light and seemed quite fragile, her power was greater than his.

Yet there was something Lutey could do. He felt in his trouser pocket and pulled out his knife. He flicked it open and held it above the water. "By the power of iron," he cried, "let me go."

Immediately the mermaid loosened her hold. "Ah, Lutey," she sighed, "you were cleverer than I thought. You knew that the power of iron is greater than all enchantments." Slowly she swam around him. "Farewell, my lovely man," she said. "Farewell for nine long years…and then we shall meet again." And saying that, she sank beneath the waves.

Lutey was trembling all over. It seemed as if his strength had been sucked out of him. But he took a deep breath, slipped his pocketknife back into its usual place, and waded toward land.

When he reached the shore, there was Towser lolloping around him, leaping up and wagging his tail and licking him all over. Lutey patted him fondly. "Good dog!" he said. "Without you I would have been lost!"

Of course, when Lutey reached his cottage, soaked to the skin, his wife was surprised.

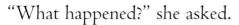

"What happened?" she asked.

"It's a long story," answered Lutey. "Wait until I'm warm and dry, and then I'll tell it."

A little later, sitting by the fire, Lutey told his wife and his wide-eyed sons about his experience with the mermaid. At the end, he took the golden comb out of his pocket.

"So it really happened," whispered his wife. "But the three wishes—I wonder, will they come true?"

They did. Lutey discovered that whenever anyone fell sick, somehow he knew what herbs and juices and powders to mix together to make the right medicine. Even his touch had healing power.

Besides this, whenever quarrels and fights broke out, people came to Lutey, and somehow he knew the truth and could make peace among them.

News of Lutey's gifts spread far and wide. Men, women, and children traveled many miles to seek his help. Lutey gave it freely, so he never grew rich. He just stayed a fisherman who loved the sea, and as his sons grew older, they too became fishermen.

Nine years passed. Nine happy years. But then, late one evening, Lutey went out fishing with Tom, his eldest son, in their small boat.

The sea was calm and still…until, without any warning, a gigantic wave came rolling toward them. Lutey and Tom held

29

on tight while the wave tossed their small boat up and down. As soon as the wave had passed, a mermaid rose up from the water. It was Morvena.

"The time has come," she sang. "Now you are mine, Lutey, my lovely man."

Slowly, silently, Lutey rose to his feet, plunged into the water, and was gone. And slowly, silently, the mermaid too sank beneath the waves. The last Tom saw of her was her

long golden hair floating across the water, and then that disappeared as well.

Lutey himself was never seen again. But from that time on, Tom, his eldest son, had the gift of healing, and he too became a peacemaker. And these gifts passed down through Lutey's family—even to this day.

But Morvena claims a high price for those gifts. Every nine years, as regularly as the sea tides, one of Lutey's descendants is lost at sea and never returns. Perhaps they all go to join Lutey and the mermaid in the enchanted world underwater. No one knows for sure.

AN ENGLISH STORY FROM CORNWALL

The Unicorn

THE UNICORN WHO WALKS ALONE

The Unicorn is a beautiful, mysterious beast who always walks alone. He is rarely seen. But once—and *only* once—the Unicorn did walk among the other animals. And that one and only time, he shared with them his strange, magical powers.

Far, far away was a wood, and under the shady trees was a pool of fresh water. It was the animals' pool, where they all came to drink.

Now, for months there had been no rain. The sun had shone, hot and fierce, drying up the streams and rivers. The grass had turned yellowy brown. Even the weeds had frizzled

up and died. But the animals' pool, under the shady trees, stayed full to the brim. And so the animals had enough water to drink.

Until, one day, a serpent came slithering out of a cave. He streaked across the dry grass, into the wood, and straight toward the animals' pool. When he reached the water's edge, he slowly raised his head and, swaying from side to side, spurted out a flood of deadly poison over the pool. It floated across the surface like oil, covering every inch. Then the serpent slithered off, as fast as he had come, back to his cave.

Why did the serpent do this? Because he was wicked. Because he felt like it. And because he cared for no one but himself. That was why.

At their usual times, the animals meandered toward the pool in ones and twos and friendly little groups. But as soon

as they reached the water's edge, they smelled the poison and saw it floating on the surface. And they knew that if they tried to drink, they would die.

The animals were distraught. Some moaned quietly. Others yelped and roared their anger. Yet not one turned and left.

By evening a huge crowd surrounded the pool. Animals who were definitely *not* good friends and who *never* drank together stood side by side: the lion, the buffalo, and the antelope; the wolf, the camel, the donkey, and the sheep…and many more besides.

The moon rose in the sky, and still more animals came. From time to time, some would call out, and then others would add their voices to the loud, mournful cry. Each time, the plaintive sounds grew louder. Was there no one who could help them?

The Unicorn, the beautiful one who walks alone, was far off, but at last he heard the animals' cries. He listened and understood they needed him. He kicked up his hooves and came trotting, slowly at first, but steadily gaining speed, until finally he was galloping faster than the wind.

As he approached the wood he slowed, and, stepping softly, he wound his way in and out among the trees. He saw the animals gathered around the pool. He smelled the poison. Then he knew everything.

The Unicorn knelt beside the pool, lowered his head, and dipped his long, pointed horn into the water, deeper and deeper, until it was completely covered. He waited a moment, then lifted his horn out of the water. He stood up. His magi-

cal horn had done its work. The poison was gone. The water was fresh and pure again.

Without pushing, nudging, or quarreling of any kind, the animals lowered their heads and drank. When their thirst was quenched and their strength returned, with one voice they all called out their thanks to the Unicorn.

But he was not there. His work done, he had departed while they were drinking. He was content always to be on his own. He was the Unicorn who walks alone.

A TRADITIONAL EUROPEAN STORY

The Thunderbird

THE GREEN-CLAWED THUNDERBIRD

Everyone is afraid of Thunderbird. Everyone hides when he comes flying. He flaps his huge wings and thunder booms. He shuts and opens his shiny eyes and lightning zigzags down to earth. He can strike trees and break them into pieces. He can strike people and cause death.

But long ago, Thunderbird was even more scary than he is now. In those times he had a terrible, *terrible* habit. He stole beautiful girls. Whenever he saw one, he would just swoop down, pick her up in his great green claws, and

carry her away to his secret home high in the mountains.

One day, in those long-ago times, a brave called Long Arrow and his lovely young wife, Red Flower, were walking beside a river. Soon big black clouds came rolling across the sky. Long Arrow and Red Flower heard the boom of distant thunder. Rain began to fall. And then they knew that Thunderbird was on his way and that they had better hide.

They ran toward their camp. They ran as fast as they could, but Thunderbird was faster. Soon he was overhead, his great wings booming out deafening thunderclaps, while lightning sizzled and flashed all around.

Thunderbird saw Red Flower, and down he swooped. He picked her up in his great green claws and flew off.

Now, the powerful lightning had stunned Long Arrow and thrown him to the ground. But he was not dead, and after a while he opened his eyes. The storm was over, and the earth smelled sweet and fresh. But where was his lovely wife? He looked all around. He saw no footprints, no signs of her leaving. And then he realized Thunderbird had taken her.

Long Arrow was sad. He turned his back on the camp and walked out into the hills so that he could be alone. Night came, but he did not sleep. He sat, still and silent, and he thought.

By the time the sun rose, Long Arrow knew what he must do. He went back to his tepee and filled a soft leather bag with food for a journey. He collected his bow and arrows. He said to his family and friends, "Thunderbird has stolen Red Flower. So now I must find the trail to his secret home, high in the mountains, and make him give back my lovely wife."

All his family, all his friends, pleaded with him: "Don't go! You can't save her! If you find him, he will surely kill you!"

But Long Arrow said nothing more and walked off toward the mountains. Because he did not know the trail that led to Thunderbird's secret home, he asked every animal he met to help him: the clever coyote, the grizzly bear, the far-flying birds, and the fearless wolf. But none of them knew the trail, either. And they also pleaded with him: "Turn back! Don't go! If you find him, he will surely kill you!"

But Long Arrow walked on. He came to the mountains and began to climb them. Halfway up the very highest one, he

came to a tepee. Raven, the wise one, was standing outside. He greeted the stranger and invited him into his tepee. There Raven spread a blanket and offered him food.

When Long Arrow had finished eating, he spoke about his lovely wife and asked Raven, the wise one, if he knew the trail to Thunderbird's secret home.

"You are close," said Raven. "He lives beside the trail that leads to the top of this mountain. His tepee is strange. It isn't made of buffalo skin. It is made of stone, and inside, hanging from the walls, are many pairs of eyes. That is where he hides the beautiful girls he has stolen—in those eyes! Only I, Raven, am greater than Thunderbird. Only I have the power to enter his tepee and live."

"Help me, Raven," said Long Arrow. "I am afraid."

"Take these," Raven said. "They are strong medicine." And he gave Long Arrow one of his big black feathers and an arrow with a shaft made of elk horn. "If you point my feather at Thunderbird, he cannot harm you. And if you shoot this arrow through the wall of his tepee, you will have power over him."

"I am still afraid," said Long Arrow.

"So—you don't believe in my strong medicine," said Raven. "Come, and I will make you believe." They walked outside, and Raven said, "Tell me how far you have traveled."

"I was sad, and I didn't count how many sleeps I had on the way," said Long Arrow. "But the trail was long. The berries on the bushes have grown and ripened since I left."

Raven gave him some ointment and told him to rub it in his eyes and then look back toward his home.

As soon as Long Arrow had done that, he called out excitedly, "I can see my camp! I can see my people, the children, the dogs, even the smoke rising up from the tepees." He turned to Raven and said, "Now I am not afraid."

Long Arrow took Raven's feather and the arrow with the elk-horn shaft and walked along the trail that led up the mountain. Just below the topmost peak, he came to what looked like an enormous tepee. But it was made of stone.

Long Arrow entered the tepee, and though it was very gloomy and dark inside, he could make out Thunderbird's huge shape sitting on the floor.

"No one enters my secret place and lives," said Thunderbird, his eyes flashing. But when he saw that Long Arrow was pointing Raven's feather toward him, Thunderbird shivered. "You hold strong medicine," he said.

"You have stolen my lovely wife, Red Flower," said Long Arrow. "And I have come for her."

"She is mine!" answered Thunderbird. "You cannot have her!"

Long Arrow fit Raven's arrow into his bow and shot it at the tepee wall. The arrow sped through the stone, making such a large hole that the sun streamed in.

Now Long Arrow could see Thunderbird's rainbow-colored feathers, his curved beak, shiny eyes, and great green claws. And Long Arrow could also see that there were many pairs of eyes hanging from the wall.

"You have Raven's power," said Thunderbird. "So I must give you what you want. Find your wife and take her."

Long Arrow recognized Red Flower's lovely eyes. He lifted the string that held them, and she stood before him, as lovely as ever.

"Do not come again to my people!" said Long Arrow. "We do not want to see or hear you!"

"But you cannot live without me," answered Thunderbird. "I make the storms of spring and summer. I bring the rain that makes the grass green and fills the berries with juice. Without the rain they would shrivel and die."

"Then come and bring us rain," said Long Arrow. "But promise not to steal our beautiful girls and not to harm any of our people with your lightning."

"Take this. It is sacred medicine," said Thunderbird. He gave Long Arrow a wooden pipe with a carved and painted stem. "When the geese come flying north in spring, you and your people must light this pipe and smoke it and pray to me. And when the smoke rises, I will remember that I must not

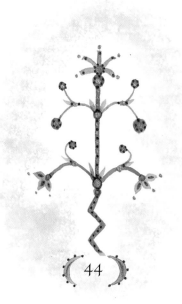

take your beautiful girls and that I must not harm your people."

Then Long Arrow took Thunderbird's medicine pipe. He and Red Flower left the secret home high on the mountain and followed the trail that led back to their camp. There were many sleeps on the way. But it did not seem far, because they were together and content.

All this happened long ago. But still, every spring, Long Arrow's descendants pray to Thunderbird, asking him not to strike any of their people with his lightning. They smoke the medicine pipe, passing it from hand to hand, and the smoke rises softly upward. And Thunderbird hears their prayers, and he answers them.

A NATIVE AMERICAN TALE

The Dragon

THE FISH AT DRAGON'S GATE

Storytellers know that China has hundreds of dragons. Every pool and river has its own dragon, and there are quite a few more in the Chinese seas. The dragons are not fierce, and they don't eat people, either—which is just as well. But *why* are there so many dragons in China?

Long ago, in China, there was a flood. It was a huge flood, like the one in the Bible, when Noah built his big boat. But in China's flood, people and animals were saved by two great heroes—magic mud and, as you might imagine, a Chinese dragon.

The Yellow Emperor, supreme god of the heavens, was angry. "People keep on doing bad, wicked things," he said. "I'm going to get rid of them! And I'm going to do it now!" So he ordered the rain god to make endless rain.

The rain god was more than happy to do this and rushed off across the sky, whipping up big black clouds and throwing down torrents of rain. He didn't stop for a moment. He loved his work.

And so, on earth, it rained endlessly, and of course there was a great flood. Houses, plants, and even trees were swept away. People and animals were drowned. A few families ran up into the mountains, hoping to survive. But even they were afraid, because every day they saw the floodwaters rise.

Only one god—Kun, grandson of the Yellow Emperor—looked down from the heavens and was truly sorry for everyone. He went to his grandfather's palace and pleaded with him. "Lord of the Heavens," he said, "stop the endless rain. Do not let any more people die."

But the Yellow Emperor was still angry. He simply closed his eyes, drew in a deep breath, and turned away.

As Kun walked out of the palace, sadly shaking his head, an old tortoise came plodding toward him.

"What's the matter?" asked the tortoise.

"I don't want any more people to drown," said Kun. "But I don't know how to help them."

"Magic mud! That's what you need!" said the tortoise. "Just sprinkle some on the floodwaters and watch what happens next!"

"Where can I get this mud?" asked Kun.

"Easy!" answered the tortoise. "The Yellow Emperor has a big jarful in his treasure-house."

"But he won't give me any," said Kun. "He doesn't want the flood to end."

"Then…" said the tortoise, and he dropped his voice to a whisper, "then…you'll have to steal some!"

Remember, Kun was a god. He had special powers. In a flash, he was inside his grandfather's treasure-house. There he found a tall jar full of soft greenish clay. He quickly took a handful and, in another flash, he was outside again.

Kun thought, and in an instant he was on earth, standing on a mountain, with the endless rain spattering down on his head.

He broke off a small piece of the mud and sprinkled it on the floodwaters. It doubled in size, doubled again, and yet again. It kept on growing, *and*, at the same time, it soaked up water like a giant sponge. Before long, the mud had made an island. Truly, it was magic mud!

Kun worked fast, traveling from place to place, sprinkling magic mud on the water, making more islands and big land bridges between the mountains. People crept out from the caves and huts where they were sheltered and watched him. At last they saw a reason to hope—perhaps the flood would not cover everything.

But still the rain fell. And besides, before Kun had used up all the mud, the Yellow Emperor looked down at the earth and saw everything.

"Kun must die!" he said, and he ordered the god of fire to do the deed.

When Kun saw the fire god coming, he changed himself into a white horse and tried to hide among some boulders at the top of a mountain. But the fire god hurled a lightning flash, and Kun, the white horse, fell down as if he were dead.

Time passed. Kun, the white horse, stirred. Something was growing inside him. He shuddered, and from out of his body sprang a new life—a golden dragon—young, strong, and splendid.

Then Kun, the brave hero, died. But his son, who called himself Yu, flew up to the heavens. He entered the palace of the Yellow Emperor, bowed his dragon head, and spoke softly and respectfully.

"Great Lord of the Heavens," he said, "I am Yu, the son of Kun, sent into the world to finish his work. Honored Great-Grandfather, the people have suffered much and are

sad. Take pity on them and stop the endless rain."

The Yellow Emperor listened. His anger cooled. "Golden Dragon," he said, "from now on you shall be the rain god. But that is not enough. I must give you some magic mud to make new land and soak up the extra water."

The Yellow Emperor pointed to a tortoise standing in a corner, listening. It was the same old tortoise who had helped Kun! "You may take as much magic mud as can be piled on top of that tortoise's back," said the Yellow Emperor, smiling.

Yu, the golden dragon, bowed his head. "I thank you, Great-Grandfather."

There was much to do. Swiftly Yu flew off. He broke up the clouds and chased and blew them away. While he was doing this, he came face-to-face with the old rain god, who was extremely angry. He had enjoyed making endless rain and didn't want to give up his job. But the Yellow Emperor had to be obeyed. All the old rain god could do was grumble and complain.

When the rain at last stopped falling, Yu piled magic mud on the tortoise's back. Then the two of them came down to earth.

Still there was much to do. Yu and the tortoise traveled through the land of China, sprinkling magic mud, making new land, and at the same time soaking up the floodwaters.

When all the magic mud had been used, Yu said to the tortoise, "Only one thing is left! We must make some rivers!"

Then, with the tortoise leading the way, the golden dragon used his tail to plow deep furrows across the soft muddy soil, from the mountains to the sea.

In most places, this was quite easy. There was only one difficult spot. When Yu was plowing the course of the Yellow River, in northern China, he came to a place where some rocky cliffs stood in the way. Yu thought for a moment, then turned around and lashed the rocks with his tail, cutting a great chasm through them.

"This place shall be called Dragon's Gate," he said. "It will always be sacred to dragons."

In this way Yu, the golden dragon, made the great rivers that flow across China today. It is also said that when the cold, sad, hungry people ventured out of the caves and huts where they had fled during the endless rain, they asked Yu to be their emperor. And so Yu, the golden dragon, became a man-god and lived on earth.

Yu is still honored and remembered, especially at Dragon's Gate on the Yellow River. There, each spring, the fish swimming upstream must leap over the fast-flowing rapids that cascade down the chasm Yu cut with his tail. The fish that leap through the wild, foaming spray and clear the rapids in one

enormous leap—those fish change into dragons and continue leaping on up into the clouds. There they frolic and play in the summertime, before returning to the rivers and pools where they sleep during the winter.

Dragons live a long, long time. Every year at Dragon's Gate, a few more dragons are born. And now you know why there are so many dragons in China.

A STORY FROM CHINA

The Sea Serpent

JAMIE AND THE BIGGEST, FIRST, AND FATHER OF ALL SEA SERPENTS

Jamie lived on a farm not far from the sea, with his mother, father, and six brothers. Because he was the youngest and smallest, everyone called him Little Jamie. They made him do the boring work no one else would do, like looking after the geese.

One day, news reached the farm that the biggest, first, and father of all sea serpents, Master Stoorworm, had come swimming from the depths of the ocean and parked himself, head to shore and tail to sea, in the next bay along the coast.

Master Stoorworm was immense. His head stuck out of the sea, big as a mountain. His two eyes were like round shiny lakes. And his body was so long that, stretched out, it could have reached across the Atlantic Ocean. Right from Europe to the shores of North America.

The monster's appetite was enormous. But he ate only breakfast. As soon as the morning sun touched his eyes, he opened his wide mouth and yawned. *"Ahhhh...,"* he sucked in fresh air, and *"Hooooo..."* he blasted out his vile breath. It smelled like rotten fish, a deadly sort of smell.

Six times Master Stoorworm yawned. The seventh time he opened his mouth, he flicked out his stretchy forked tongue, scooped up an enormous breakfast, and flung it into his mouth. This tongue was so powerful it could knock down a house and grab the people inside. It could sweep up half a dozen cows or a boat full of fishermen. But most frightening of all—this tongue was so long it was not possible to guess where the monster would strike next. No one was safe.

When Jamie's mother heard about Master Stoorworm, she said, "Something must be done!"

"Someone," said his father, "will have to kill him!"

"I'll fight him," said Jamie, who was toasting his toes by the fire. "I'm not scared."

His six brothers laughed out loud and started to tease. "Little Jamie!" they shouted. "Our little brother! The *big* hero!"

Now, King Harald, the ruler of that country, was an old man with a wise head on his shoulders. He called a meeting of The Thing, which was a special council that met to make laws and govern. And the king told the council that a brave champion must be found to kill Master Stoorworm.

This announcement set off a babble of voices.

"He can't be killed!" said one. "Waste of time trying!"

"Somehow we must keep him happy!" said another.

"We could feed him tasty morsels," said a third. "Seven lovely maidens, tied up on the rocks every morning…or maybe a princess. Then the monster would leave the rest of us in peace."

"Wait!" said the king. "Wait seven more days. A champion may be found. And if he does kill Master Stoorworm, he can marry my only child, Princess Gem-de-Lovely, and inherit my kingdom. He shall also have my precious sword, Sicker Snapper, which was given to me by the god Odin himself."

News of the king's prize—a princess, a kingdom, and a sword—spread throughout the land and beyond. And so, seven days later, about midday, a large crowd gathered by the seashore to see if a hero could be found. Jamie and his family were there, along with the king, his lovely daughter, all the members of The Thing, and thirty-six tough-looking champion fighters.

Some of the champions had plans, and some had not the least idea what they were going to do. But they all swaggered about, looking brave—until Master Stoorworm opened his mouth and yawned a sleepy, after-breakfast yawn. *"Ahhhhh…"*

Whew! The smell of his breath was vile. Twelve champions fainted on the spot, twelve got sick, and the last twelve clamped their fingers over their noses and ran.

"I see there are no champions left!" said King Harald. "So, tomorrow, before Master Stoorworm wakes, I shall come myself and fight him."

"You are too old, my lord," said his chief steward. "Your fighting days are over."

The king drew out his precious sword, Sicker Snapper. "On this sword, I tell you all that I will die myself before my daughter or any other maiden is offered to the monster." He turned to his chief steward and said, "Prepare a boat with two stout oars, mast up, and sail ready to hoist. Order the boatman to guard it till I come tomorrow before sunrise."

On their way home Jamie said, "I'd fight Master Stoorworm. Really I would. I'm not scared."

His brothers laughed. "*Little* Jamie! The *big* hero!" they shouted, and, catching hold of him, rolled him on the ground in a rough-and-tumble way—six against one—until their father stopped them.

When Jamie got to his feet, he stuck his chin in the air. "I could have beaten the lot of you!" he said. "But I am saving my strength—for Master Stoorworm!"

That night Jamie lay quietly in his bed, thinking over his plans. He was going to fight Master Stoorworm.

As soon as everyone else was fast asleep, he crept outside, mounted his father's horse, and galloped off. The moon was full and the sky starry bright, so Jamie easily found the path that led to the seashore.

When he came to a small, one-room cottage, he jumped off the horse, tethered him to the gatepost, and opened the door. Jamie's old granny lay in bed, snoring. The peat fire was banked up, and on the floor beside it stood an iron pot. Jamie bent over, picked up a glowing piece of peat from the fire, and placed it in the pot. Then he crept out as softly as he had come. His granny heard nothing. Only the gray cat at the bottom of her bed looked up and stretched.

King Harald's boat was ready, mast up and afloat in the shallow water. The boatman sat in it, swinging his arms across his chest to warm himself.

Jamie called out, "It's a rare nippy morning! Why don't you take a run on the shore and warm yourself?"

"Leave the boat? I wouldn't dare!" the boatman called back. "The chief steward would have me beaten black and blue if anything happened to the king's boat today!"

Jamie put down the iron pot and began poking around in a rock pool, as if he were collecting shellfish. Suddenly he jumped up and yelled out: "Gold! Gold! Yes! It's bright as the sun! It must be gold!"

This was too much for the boatman. Quick as he could, he was out of the boat, across the sands, and down on his knees by the rock pool, looking for gold. And Jamie? He picked up the pot with the live peat in it, skipped lightly across the sands, and untied the boat rope. Then he jumped aboard, grabbed hold of an oar, and pushed off.

By the time the boatman looked up, Jamie was out at sea with sail up, the boat flying. The boatman was furious. He waved his arms and yelled the angriest, rudest words he could think of. But there was nothing he could do.

When King Harald, his chief steward, the princess, and their servants arrived, they too were furious. And when a whole crowd of curious folk gathered, including Jamie's fam-

ily, they were not pleased, either. But what could they do? Nothing but wait and watch. Meanwhile, Jamie pointed the small boat toward Master Stoorworm's mountainous head and sailed on. When he came close, he jammed the boat up against the monster's mouth, took down the sail, and pulled in the oars. After that, he waited.

The sun, round and red, rose slowly above a distant valley. Its bright rays struck Master Stoorworm's two big eyes and woke him up. He stretched his wide mouth open and began the first of the seven yawns that he yawned each morning before breakfast.

Now, as Master Stoorworm breathed in, a flood of seawater swept into his mouth and down his throat. Jamie and the boat were sucked in with it. On and on, faster and faster, they were carried down the monster's throat, which was softly lit, here and there, by a silvery, phosphorescent light.

At last the water became shallower, and the boat came to rest. Jamie lifted the iron pot, jumped out of the boat, and ran

until he came to the monster's liver. He pulled a knife out of his pocket and cut a hole in the oily liver. Then he stuffed the glowing peat into the hole. He blew and blew until he thought his lips would crack. But, finally, the peat burst into flame, the oil in the liver hissed and sputtered, there was a flash, and Master Stoorworm's liver was ablaze.

Jamie ran back to the boat as fast as he could. He jumped in and held tight—just in time, too. When Master Stoorworm felt the fierce heat of the fire inside him, he twisted and turned and thrashed about with such violence that he threw up. The entire contents of the monster's enormous stomach shot up his throat in a torrent, catching hold of the boat and sweeping it along, up and out of his mouth, across the sea, till it landed, high and dry, on a sand dune.

No one even noticed Jamie! The king and everyone else who had come to watch—and that included Jamie's granny and the gray cat who had looked up and stretched—all ran off to the top of the nearest hill.

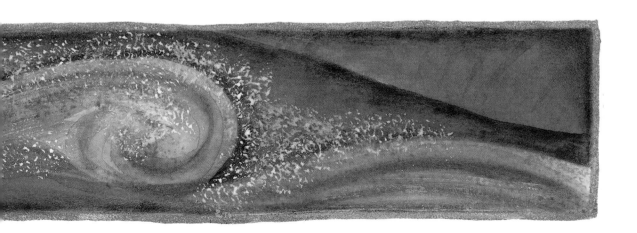

Jamie was out of the boat in a moment and soon chasing after them, trying to escape the huge waves that were crashing ashore as Master Stoorworm thrashed and thundered and writhed.

By now the monster was more to be pitied than feared. Black clouds of smoke were belching out of his mouth and nostrils as the fire inside him grew fiercer. He tossed to and fro. He flung out his forked tongue and stretched it, up and up, toward the cool sky. He tossed his head, and his tongue fell down so hard it made a huge dent in the earth. The sea rushed in, and that dent became the crooked straits that now separate Denmark from Norway and Sweden.

Master Stoorworm drew in his tongue and this time flung his whole head up and up toward the cool sky. He twisted and turned, and his head came down so hard and fast that some of his teeth fell out and landed in the sea. And they became the scattered islands that are now called the Orkney Islands.

Again his head rose. He tossed it up and up, and when it came down this time, even more teeth fell out. And they became the Shetland Islands.

A third time the great head rose up, and when it came down this time, all the rest of his teeth fell out. And they became the Faroe Islands.

After that Master Stoorworm coiled himself around and around into a great lump and died. This lump became Iceland, and the fire that Jamie lit with the burning peat still burns beneath that land. Even today, there are mountains in Iceland that spew out fire.

When everyone was absolutely certain Master Stoorworm was dead, King Harald could scarcely contain himself. He threw his arms around Jamie and called him his son. He took off his royal cloak and put it on Jamie and gave him his precious sword, Sicker Snapper. And then the king took hold of the princess's hand and put it in Jamie's.

Of course, a wedding followed—and such a wedding! The feasting and dancing lasted for nine whole weeks. Everyone was happy because Master Stoorworm was dead and they could now live in peace. And everyone, Jamie's brothers included, agreed that Jamie was their champion—a *big* hero!

A SCANDINAVIAN STORY TOLD IN THE ORKNEY ISLANDS

The Feathered Snake

HOW MUSIC CAME TO THE WORLD

In the beginning times, the earth had no music. No one knew how to sing. Not even the birds. But there *was* music far away and high above, in the House of the Sun.

One day the great god Smoking Mirror came to earth and walked about, examining the things he had helped to make.

"Very good! Everything looks just the way I wanted," he said. "The flowers, the birds, the animals! Bright colors everywhere! And yet…I feel something is missing." He listened. He walked on and listened some more. "I know what's missing," he said.

He threw back his head and hurled his voice to the four corners of the earth. "Come, Quetzalcoatl, feathered snake, restless Lord of the Winds! Come! I need you!"

Quetzalcoatl was a long way off, drifting lazily above the waves. Nevertheless, he heard. He lifted his snake head and opened his mouth wide, until a human face appeared within his jaws. It was a rather grumpy face.

"The same old story," he grumbled. "Just when I'm enjoying a rest, I'm summoned for something or other. Still, I suppose I must go and find out what's the matter now!"

He gathered himself together, his glossy feathers rippling around him, changing color—now green, now turquoise, now blue. Then he came flying.

Fast, faster than fast, he flew. Waves rose high. They crashed against the shore. Trees lifted their branches and tossed them to and fro. In a great whoosh of sound, he landed beside Smoking Mirror.

"So—what do you want?" asked Quetzalcoatl. He was brisk and sharp. Those two were not always friends. It didn't take much for them to quarrel.

But Smoking Mirror was cunning. He spoke softly, flatteringly. "Lord of the Winds, there is work that only you can do."

"*Work!*" Quetzalcoatl howled out the word. "I wouldn't have come if—"

"Listen," said Smoking Mirror. "This bright earth we made together is sick. Listen. Can't you hear? There is no music. And what is life without music? The earth *must* have music. So,

feathered snake, great Lord of the Winds, you must go to the House of the Sun and bring some music down to the earth."

"Go to the sun! Go and get music!" exclaimed Quetzalcoatl. "You know the sun. He loves music. But he's mean. He won't share. He wants every note of music and every single musician for himself alone!"

"But think of the birds, the trees, and the moving water," said Smoking Mirror. "Think of the mothers with their babies, lively children, sleepy children, grown men and women. They must have music. All life should be full of music!"

Quetzalcoatl thought. "I will go," he said. "I will go to the House of the Sun."

He gathered himself together and flew upward. He soared through the blue smoke of the sky and on through the empty space. Up and up he flew, until he came to the roof of the world, and there he heard the sound of distant music. As he ascended the stairway of light that led to the House of the Sun, the music grew louder and louder, until he was filled with the glorious sound of huge choirs singing and sweet flutes playing.

At last he entered the House of the Sun and beheld a splendid sight.

Musicians circled the sun in a sphere of light. There was not a dark color anywhere. Each musician was dressed according to the music played. Those who sang lullabies and other songs for children wore white. Those who sang tender love songs wore deep blue. The ones who sang loud songs about brave deeds and battles were dressed in red. But brightest of all were the flute players, who were dressed in a golden color that gleamed like the sun himself.

The music wove in and out and around the sphere of light, as first one group sang and then another sang or played their flutes. The glorious sounds never stopped, not for a moment.

As soon as the sun saw Quetzalcoatl, he knew why he had come.

"Musicians, be quiet!" the sun ordered. "Here comes that bothersome nuisance, the feathered one! Don't answer when he speaks, or he'll steal you away and take you to that terrible, dark, sad place called earth, where there is no music."

For the first time the musicians fell silent. They were afraid. They tried not to listen as Quetzalcoatl drifted among them, whispering in their ears: "Take pity on the people of earth. Come with me, and teach them how to make music. Come…"

Over and over he pleaded with them, but the musicians stood still and silent as statues.

Quetzalcoatl's anger surged up. He coiled and uncoiled himself. He piled up black storm clouds until they completely covered the sun's own light. He brewed up a hurricane. Lightning flashed. Thunder rumbled and roared.

The musicians were terrified now! They had never known darkness like this before, and they had never been at the center of a storm. They ran this way and that, trying to find the sun. Some, not knowing where they were going, ran straight into Quetzalcoatl's feathered embrace.

When he had hold of musicians of every kind, he wound his body around them and slowly, gently, so as not to harm them, floated down to earth.

Smoking Mirror was there to welcome them as they landed.

"Quetzalcoatl," he said, "you have brought such a marvelous flutter of happiness to earth!"

The musicians were relieved when they saw that the earth was not a terrible, dark place after all. It was full of bright colors, and they could still see the sun, shining above them. True, there was no music, but they would change that.

Swiftly they walked off to the four corners of the earth. On their way they taught everyone they met how to sing or how to make flutes and play them.

They also taught the birds to warble and showed them how to greet the sun each morning in a loud dawn chorus. They gave music to the moving water and the rustling leaves. They even taught Quetzalcoatl, Lord of the Winds, how to whistle and sigh and hum.

And so now, today, all the earth everywhere is full of the happiness that music brings!

A STORY FROM CENTRAL AMERICA AND MEXICO

The Minotaur

THE ONE AND ONLY MINOTAUR

Long ago, on the island of Crete, there lived the Minotaur—the one and only Minotaur. There has never been another. He was a most ferocious beast, half man, half bull, and he fed on human flesh.

King Minos, the ruler of Crete, kept the Minotaur in a vast maze called the Labyrinth, which had been specially built underneath the royal palace. It was a terrible place—so dark and such a mass of twisting, turning passages that it was impossible for anyone who went in ever to find his way out.

Back then, King Minos was all-powerful in the world of the Mediterranean. In order to feed the ferocious Minotaur, he passed a grim law. Every nine years, Aegeus, king of Athens, must send to Crete seven lads and seven young girls who would be thrust into the Labyrinth, one by one.

Twice, young lads and girls were sent. The third time came round. It was springtime. The sun shone, the birds sang, and the almond trees blossomed in pink. But in Athens there was sadness. The time had come for the city to draw lots to choose seven lads and seven young girls and send them to Crete.

Now, Aegeus was an old man and very frail. But he had an only son called Theseus, who was handsome, tall, strong, and fleet-footed. And the king loved his only son with a great love.

On the morning when the lots were to be drawn, the king, his son, and the citizens of Athens gathered in front of the palace. Some were silent. Some wept. Others whispered prayers to the gods: "Not my son! Not my daughter! Don't let them be chosen!"

When Theseus saw how sad everyone was, he said to his father, "I must go to Crete and try to kill this Minotaur!"

"No—don't go!" said the king. "It would mean certain death. You can't kill this beast alone and unarmed. And even if you did, you'd never find your way out of the terrible Labyrinth."

But Theseus turned to the crowd. "Lots will be drawn for only six young lads," he said. "I shall be the seventh. And, you can be sure, I shall try to kill the Minotaur!"

"Ohhhh…" There was a long, low gasp. Everyone was full of admiration that Theseus, the king's only son, should freely offer to go.

When the lots were drawn and the seven girls and six lads chosen, Theseus gathered the young people around him. "Be brave," he said. "Always have hope. The Minotaur can't live forever!" Then he led them down to the harbor, followed by their weeping mothers and fathers, sisters, and brothers.

Just before Theseus boarded the ship that was to take him to Crete, King Aegeus put his arms about his son. "Theseus, promise me one thing," he said. "The ship is rigged with the black sails of death. Now, if you are on board when it returns, take down the black sails and hoist white ones in their place. Then, even from a long way off, I shall know that you are alive and safe."

Theseus promised he would do this.

A few days later, Theseus and his companions arrived at Knossos, the chief city of Crete. Armed guards met them and took them along steep paths, up stone steps, and into the immense royal palace spread out high on a hill.

They entered a beautiful room where every wall was covered with bright painted pictures. There, seated on his throne, was King Minos with his two daughters, Phaedra and Ariadne, on either side.

Thirteen prisoners stood with bowed heads. Only Theseus stood straight and tall and looked directly at King Minos.

"Bold youth," said the king, "who are you?"

"I am Theseus, son of Aegeus, king of Athens," he answered. "And I have come to kill the Minotaur so that no more of our young people need die!"

Then the king ordered the guards to search Theseus. And when they found that he carried no weapons, King Minos laughed. "How will you kill the Minotaur?" he asked. "With your hands?"

"If I must!" answered Theseus.

Ariadne, the princess, looked at Theseus. He was so brave, so strong. "I will help him," she thought. "A man like this ought not to die!"

As soon as the young Athenians were taken away to the palace prison, Ariadne went to the kitchens and stirred sleeping powders into some large jugs of wine. She ordered servants to give the wine to the prison guards.

Then she went to her father's room and stole a fine sharp sword.

Finally, she opened a small painted box in which she kept her private treasures and took out a ball of golden thread. Ariadne had told no one about this ball, not even her sister. It

had been given to her when she was a little girl by clever Daedalus, the man who had designed and built the Labyrinth. He had said, "Play with the glittering ball, Ariadne. But don't forget. It has magic...." And he whispered something in her ear.

That night the guards, of course, slept soundly! And so did the prisoners, who were tired from their journey. But Theseus lay awake, trying to work out how he could kill the Minotaur.

About midnight the prison door swung open, and there stood Ariadne, the princess. "Come," she said. "Follow me."

She took Theseus along winding corridors and down long stairways. At last she unlocked a heavy wooden door and opened it. In front of them was a narrow passage—and beyond it? Theseus could see only darkness beyond. They were at the entrance to the Labyrinth.

Then Ariadne gave Theseus her father's sword. "With this you can kill the Minotaur," she said. She gave him the ball of golden thread as well, but she held on to the loose end herself. "Place the ball on the floor," she said. "It will roll forward of its own accord and guide you to the center of the Labyrinth. When you return, wind it up, and it will guide you out."

"And will you wait here till I return?" asked Theseus.

"I shall hold my end of the thread, and I shall wait!" said Ariadne.

Theseus placed the golden ball on the floor, and as it rolled off into the darkness, the thread glowed, giving out a hazy sort of light. He followed it along cold, narrow stone passages. He turned to the right, then the left, twisted back, and turned again, always following the ball.

He walked on until the golden ball came to rest in a large, gray, shadowy space. Theseus had reached the heart of the Labyrinth, and there, as if waiting for him, was the Minotaur.

The ferocious beast swung his massive head from side to side. He snorted and stamped his feet. Then, lowering his shoulders, his horns pointing forward as sharp as daggers, he charged.

Theseus gripped the sword and stood his ground. The Minotaur was almost upon him. But at the last moment, in one swift movement, Theseus leaped aside and thrust the sword into the monster's neck. The beast stumbled, slowly fell to the floor, and died.

Now Theseus had to escape from the Labyrinth. He saw the golden ball glowing hazily in a shadowy space. He picked it up and set off, winding the thread around the ball as he went. By the same twisting, turning route, it led him back to the open door and to Ariadne.

Then everything happened quickly. Theseus and Ariadne woke his young companions and guided them out of the palace. On the way to the harbor, Ariadne decided to leave also. She liked Theseus and wanted to be with him. And besides, she knew her father would be angry when he found out what she had done.

So they all boarded the Athenian ship. The sailors were shaken awake, and the black sails were hoisted. Then—one final deed—before they left Crete, Theseus and the young lads set fire to King Minos's largest and swiftest ships so that the king would not be able to chase after them.

After several days at sea, a gale blew up and the waves became wild and choppy. Poor Ariadne grew seasick. She felt so ill that all she wanted to do was to leave the ship as soon as possible.

She pleaded with Theseus, and in the end he ordered the sailors to make for the nearest island and put her ashore. Before she stepped onto dry land, Ariadne and Theseus said fond farewells. But that was the end of their friendship. They never saw each other again.

Perhaps it was because of the rough seas and the sadness of Ariadne leaving—who knows? Anyway, somehow Theseus did not remember his promise to his father. He forgot to order the sailors to take down the black sails and hoist white ones in their place.

Day after day, old King Aegeus had watched from the top of the cliffs, waiting for the return of the ship that had taken Theseus to Crete. When one morning he saw a ship approaching with black sails billowing in the wind, he thought his only son was dead. Overwhelmed by sorrow, the king flung himself into the sea and drowned.

When Theseus's ship finally put down anchor and he and the six lads and seven young girls came ashore, there was great joy in Athens.

"Theseus, our hero!" the people cried. "You have killed the Minotaur! You have saved our children!" And they hung garlands of flowers around his neck.

For a very short while Theseus was happy. But then a messenger arrived with news of his father's death.

Theseus's eyes filled with tears. "The sails—the black sails!" he cried. "How could I have forgotten?" But the deed was done. It couldn't be changed.

So Theseus became king of Athens, and he was a good king, wise and strong, and loved by all his people.

But he never forgot his father, who had loved him with such a great love. And, in his honor, Theseus decided to call the sea where King Aegeus had drowned the Aegean. And so it has remained. Look on any map and you will find that the wide waters to the east of Athens are still called the Aegean Sea.

A GREEK MYTH

The Naga

THREE FABULOUS EGGS

Once, long ago, the King of the Nagas and his daughter, the Naga Princess, lived in a magnificent underwater palace hidden in a deep lake among the hills of northern Burma.

Sometimes the Naga Princess took the shape of a hooded cobra. Sometimes she was half woman, half snake. But often she walked beside the lake or along forest paths as a beautiful young woman dressed in showy, bright-colored clothes. She wore a velvet skirt and leggings and a velvet top. Rising up over her head was a glorious hood, all set with sparkling rubies.

One day when the Naga Princess was walking beside the lake, the Sun Prince glanced down from the sky and saw her. He was thrilled by her brilliant appearance. He couldn't keep his eyes off her.

"She is so beautiful," he thought. "I must speak with her and find out who she is."

In a moment the Sun Prince came down and stood beside her. The Naga Princess was not surprised. She turned her calm, gentle eyes toward the handsome stranger. They talked together, and a strong love grew between them. Before long, they decided to marry.

For a while they lived together in quiet happiness. Then one morning the Sun Prince remembered that he had work to do.

"I must return to my father, the sun, and help him light the world," he said. "So come with me, my Naga Princess."

She slowly shook her head. "I cannot leave these shady forests and my own cool lake. I cannot live in the sky."

"Then every day I will look down and watch you," said the Sun Prince. "If at any time you need me, send a white crow with a message." With that, he was gone.

The Naga Princess was sad and lonely without her husband. Day after day she looked up, and when she saw his father, the sun, she thought of her handsome Sun Prince.

But then something wonderful happened. The Naga Princess laid three eggs. Three fabulous eggs. They were ruby red, like her favorite jewel, and streaked with gold from their father, the Sun Prince. She covered the eggs with leaves and guarded them carefully. At last she was happy again.

One morning, when the eggs were almost ready to hatch,

she heard a harsh *Caw! Caw!* A crow was perched on a nearby tree. He was a white crow, of course, because in those days there were no black ones.

"Crow, will you be my messenger?" said the Naga Princess. "Will you fly up to the sky and ask the Sun Prince to come and see his three children who are soon to be hatched?"

"I'll do that!" said the crow.

"But don't stop on the way!" warned the Naga Princess.

"As if I would!" replied the crow, and off he flew.

It was a long way to the Sun Prince, but in the end the crow reached him.

"Three children! Such good news!" exclaimed the Sun Prince. "But"—and he sighed—"I cannot leave my work. Not now. I'm busy. Still, I shall send my Naga Princess a present."

He searched his father's treasure-house until he found a very large, dazzling ruby. "Her favorite jewel. It will be the perfect gift," he murmured as he wrapped it carefully in a piece of golden silk and tied up the ends.

"Tell my Naga Princess that I cannot visit her and my children for a while," said the Sun Prince. "But I want her to have this precious ruby as a token of my love."

"I'll do that!" the crow assured him.

"But don't stop on the way!" warned the Sun Prince.

"As if I would!" replied the crow, and off he flew.

It was a long way, but in the end he reached the hills of northern Burma.

He was almost back home when what should he see but some merchants sitting on the ground in a forest clearing.

They were eating their supper and throwing the leftovers to some birds who were flying around, swooping and diving and noisily quarreling over the food.

Now, the crow had flown a long way, and he was hungry. He didn't think twice about his promise. He flew down, hopped under a bush, dropped his precious bundle, and came fluttering out to join the other birds for leftovers.

It happened that one of the merchants had seen the bird drop the bundle. Since it looked like gold, the merchant hurried over to the bush, picked up

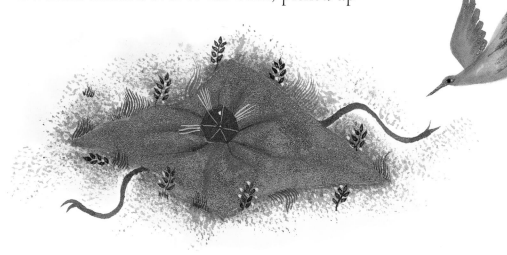

the bundle, and untied the piece of golden silk.

"A ruby!" he gasped. "So big! So dazzling! It must be worth a fortune!" Quickly he slipped the jewel into his pocket. "I had better put something else in its place," he thought.

He looked around. Nearby was a piece of dried-up cow dung about the same size as the dazzling ruby. So—what did he do but put the dried-up cow dung inside the cloth before tying it up again.

The crow hadn't seen any of this. He was too busy eating. At last, when he was sure he was absolutely full, he hopped over to the bush, picked up the bundle, and flew off.

The Naga Princess was overjoyed when the white crow returned and dropped a small bundle wrapped in golden silk into her open hands.

"The Sun Prince is busy," explained the crow, who was feeling proud and very important. "He cannot visit you now but has sent this present as a token of his love."

What could it be? The Naga Princess was so excited, her fingers trembled as she opened the bundle. But when she saw the dried-up piece of cow dung, she flung it to the ground, and her eyes flared with anger.

"Did you stop on the way?" she asked.

"As if I would!" replied the crow. He half guessed what had happened. But was he going to get himself into trouble? Not this crow. "As if I would!" he repeated, and off he flew as fast as he could.

The Naga Princess, who was usually so quiet and gentle, now raged with anger. She never wanted to see the Sun Prince again! And the three fabulous eggs? She uncovered them, summoned all her anger into her eyes, and glared at them. They were her children. She would not destroy them. She would not turn them to ashes as she could have.

But still she glared at them, until all the anger had flowed right out of her and into those eggs.

Then she dived into the lake, changed into a snake-woman, and swam back to her father's underwater palace. She had decided never again to live on land. From now on she would remain in her underwater home.

It has to be said that the Sun Prince was careless. He was so busy working that he forgot to look down and watch the Naga Princess every day. However, a time came when he did look, and he couldn't find her. He looked by the lake and along her favorite paths, and still he couldn't see her.

He looked throughout the land of Burma, until his eyes rested on a busy marketplace. There he saw a merchant holding a dazzling ruby in his hands. It was the very ruby that came from the treasure-house of the sun.

The Sun Prince knew immediately that the crow must have stopped on the way to the Naga Princess. "I will punish him!" the Sun Prince vowed.

So he blazed fierce sun rays straight at the very first white crow he saw. He scorched the white feathers until they turned charcoal black. The Sun Prince saw another white crow, and he scorched its feathers, too. The Sun Prince scorched the feathers of every white crow he could find.

And that is why there are no longer any white crows in Burma. They are all charcoal black.

Now, you must wonder, what happened to the three eggs?

First, until the rainy season, they just lay where the Naga Princess had left them. Then water came gushing down the hillside and washed the three eggs into a stream. The stream carried them into a big river, where they were bounced and tossed and swept along in the swirling water.

The eggs reached the town of Mogok, and one of them was flung against a rock. When it burst open, hundreds of dazzling rubies came cascading out. And, from that day to this, rubies can be found near the town of Mogok.

The two remaining eggs were swept along into the great Irrawaddy River, where one of the eggs was flung against a rock. When it burst open, a tiger came leaping and snarling out of the egg. And, from that day to this, the most ferocious tigers in the world can be found in the jungles of Burma.

The remaining egg was swept along, and, just before the Irrawaddy River reaches the sea, this egg too was flung against a rock. When it burst open, a crocodile came crawling out, snapping its jaws. And from that day to this, hungry crocodiles can be found lurking in all the shallow creeks and rivers of Lower Burma.

So it is that the rubies, the tigers, and the crocodiles of Burma are brothers and sisters. They are all the children of the Sun Prince and his beautiful wife, the Naga Princess.

A STORY FROM BURMA

The Phoenix

BIRD OF THE SUN

There is a bird that lays no eggs and has no young. It was here when the world began and is still living today, in a hidden, faraway desert spot. It is the Phoenix, the bird of fire.

One day, in the beginning times, the sun looked down and saw a large bird with shimmering feathers. They were red and gold—bright and dazzling like the sun itself. The sun called out, "Glorious Phoenix, you shall be my bird and live forever!"

Live forever! The Phoenix was overjoyed to hear these words. It lifted its head and sang, "Sun, glorious sun, I shall sing my songs for you alone!"

But the Phoenix was not happy for long. Poor bird. Its feathers were far too beautiful. Men, women, and children were always chasing it and trying to trap it. They wanted to have some of those beautiful, shiny feathers for themselves.

"I cannot live here," thought the Phoenix. And it flew off toward the east, where the sun rises in the morning.

The Phoenix flew for a long time, and then it came to a far-away, hidden desert where no humans lived. And there the Phoenix remained in peace, flying freely and singing its songs of praise to the sun above.

Almost five hundred years passed. The Phoenix was still alive, but it had grown old. It was often tired, and it had lost much of its strength. It couldn't soar so high in the sky, nor fly as fast or as far as when it was young.

"I don't want to live like this," thought the Phoenix. "I want to be young and strong."

So the Phoenix lifted its head and sang, "Sun, glorious sun, make me young and strong again!" But the sun didn't answer. Day after day the Phoenix sang. When the sun still didn't answer, the Phoenix decided to return to the place where it had lived in the beginning and ask the sun one more time.

It flew across the desert, over hills, green valleys, and high mountains. The journey was long, and because the Phoenix was old and weak, it had to rest along the way. Now, the Phoenix has a keen sense of smell and is particularly fond of herbs and spices. So each time it landed, it collected pieces of cinnamon bark and all kinds of fragrant leaves. It tucked some in among its feathers and carried the rest in its claws.

When at last the bird came to the place that had once been its home, it landed on a tall palm tree growing high on a mountainside. Right at the top of the tree, the Phoenix built a nest with the cinnamon bark and lined it with the fragrant leaves. Then the Phoenix flew off and collected some sharp-scented gum called myrrh, which it had seen oozing out of a nearby tree. The Phoenix made an egg from the myrrh and carried the egg back to the nest.

Now everything was ready. The Phoenix sat down in its nest, lifted its head, and sang, "Sun, glorious sun, make me young and strong again!"

This time the sun heard the song. Swiftly it chased the clouds from the sky and stilled the winds and shone down on the mountainside with all its power.

The animals, the snakes, the lizards, and every other bird hid from the sun's fierce rays—in caves and holes, under shady rocks and trees. Only the Phoenix sat upon its nest and let the sun's rays beat down upon its beautiful, shiny feathers.

Suddenly there was a flash of light, flames leaped out of the nest, and the Phoenix became a big round blaze of fire.

After a while the flames died down. The tree was not burnt, nor was the nest. But the Phoenix was gone. In the nest was a heap of silvery-gray ash.

The ash began to tremble and slowly heave itself upward. From under the ash there rose up a young Phoenix. It was small and looked sort of crumpled, but it stretched its neck and lifted its wings and flapped them. Moment by moment it grew, until it was the same size as the old Phoenix. It looked around, found the egg made of myrrh, and hollowed it out. Then it placed the ashes inside and finally closed up the egg. The young Phoenix lifted its head and sang, "Sun, glorious sun, I shall sing my songs for you alone! Forever and ever!"

When the song ended, the wind began to blow, the clouds came scudding across the sky, and the other living creatures crept out of their hiding places.

Then the Phoenix, with the egg in its claws, flew up and away. At the same time, a cloud of birds of all shapes and sizes rose up from the earth and flew behind the Phoenix, singing together, "You are the greatest of birds! You are our king!"

The birds flew with the Phoenix to the temple of the sun that the Egyptians had built at Heliopolis, city of the sun. Then the Phoenix placed the egg with the ashes inside on the sun's altar.

"Now," said the Phoenix, "I must fly on alone." And, while the other birds watched, it flew off toward the faraway desert.

The Phoenix lives there still. But every five hundred years, when it begins to feel weak and old, it flies west to the same mountain. There it builds a fragrant nest on top of a palm tree, and there the sun once again burns it to ashes. But each time, the Phoenix rises up from those ashes, fresh and new and young again.

AN EGYPTIAN STORY

More About the Stories

THE HORSE THAT COULD FLY

Sometimes the fire-breathing Chimera is described as having just two heads—a lion's and a snake's—on a goat's body. Even so, she is such an unlikely-looking creature that her name is used in the English language to describe a wild, foolish dream or fantasy. In Greek myths she has two equally strange relatives. One is Cerberus, a three-headed hound with a snake's tail, who guards Hades, Land of the Dead. The other is the Hydra, a water monster with a whole lot of snaky heads. The big problem with the Hydra is that if one head is cut off, another two or maybe three sprout up in its place. See Robert Graves, *The Greek Myths* (2 vols.), 1955.

The great mass of wonderful stories we call Greek myths were first written down over 2,500 years ago. But some of the stories and some of the fabulous beasts, such as the winged horse and the Chimera, have their origins in earlier civilizations of the Near East.

DON'T EVER LOOK AT A MERMAID

Reported sightings of a real, live mermaid were quite common among European sailors until about a hundred years ago. The mermaid was usually sitting alone on a rock, combing her long flowing hair, or swimming among the waves.

The mermaid is always dangerous. She can easily bewitch a man with her beauty and sweet singing and then lure him to her underwater home, a place full of treasures. Mermen, on the other hand, are cross and ugly, not particularly interested in humans and not often seen. But if a mermaid is harmed, mermen will raise storms and wreck ships.

This story is retold by Robert Hunt, *Popular Romances of the West of England*, 1865, and William Bottrell, *Traditional and Hearthside Stories of West Cornwall*, 1870.

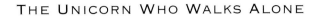

The Unicorn Who Walks Alone

The earliest surviving description of a Unicorn was written about 400 B.C. by Ctesias, a Greek physician who had traveled with the king of Persia. He wrote that, in India, there were swift wild asses with white bodies, dark red heads, and a pointed horn in the middle of the forehead. This horn was about twenty inches long and white at the base, black in the middle, and bright crimson at the top. Any cup made from the horn would protect the drinker from poison. During the Middle Ages, particularly in Western Europe, belief that the horn could be used against poison resulted in a lively trade in what were thought to be Unicorn horns. Most of these were probably tusks of a sea mammal, the narwhal. In 1605 one horn was bought for 12,000 gold pieces.

This story began its life in a bestiary—a book of facts and fables about real and imaginary animals. Bestiaries were popular with Christians from about the third century onward. This tale is retold by Odell Shepard, *The Lore of the Unicorn*, 1930.

Over the centuries, writers and, more especially, artists have changed the Unicorn. He has become all white, more goatlike, and less horselike. The horn has grown longer, changed to black, then white, and developed spiral markings.

The Green-Clawed Thunderbird

The idea that thunder was caused by a bird flapping its great wings, and lightning caused by its blinking its eyes, was widespread among Native American tribes of the Pacific Northwest and of the plateaus, the plains, and the northeastern woodlands.

Some believed there was a flock or family of Thunderbirds, while others believed there was one enormous bird. Along the Pacific coast, it was thought to be so strong it could lift a large whale out of the ocean and carry it ashore. According to a tradition of the Blackfoot (a northern Plains tribe), a Thunderbird was once overcome by a snowstorm and landed in a camp, and the people saw that its feathers had many colors, like the rainbow, and its claws were long and green.

The story is retold by G. B. Grinnell, *Blackfoot Lodge Tales*, 1893.

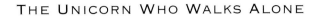

THE FISH AT DRAGON'S GATE

The Chinese dragon has a head like a camel, two horns, and whiskers at the sides of its mouth. It carries a precious pearl under its chin or in its mouth. Like the European folktale dragon, it has scales, four legs, claws, a hoard of treasure, and it can fly. But it usually has no wings; it does not eat beautiful young girls; and it breathes out misty clouds, not fire or deadly fumes. It sleeps in pools, rivers, or even the sea in winter. In spring it wakes and flies up to the sky, where all dragons gather to fight and play and make the summer rain. Sometimes they stay up too long, and the rains are then so heavy that there are floods.

The story is based on material by Yüan Ke (selected and translated by K. Echlin and N. Zhixiong), *Dragons and Dynasties: An Introduction to Chinese Mythology*, 1993, and Anne Birrell, *Chinese Mythology: An Introduction*, 1993.

JAMIE AND THE BIGGEST, FIRST, AND FATHER OF ALL SEA SERPENTS

According to Scandinavian mythology, an immense serpent lies beneath the sea, curled around the earth, tail in mouth. It will break loose when the world ends. Then Thor, god of thunder, will fight it, but fate has decided that the serpent's poisonous fumes will finally kill the god.

The story of Master Stoorworm comes from the Orkney Islands, which, like the Shetland Islands, have a rich heritage of stories and beliefs from their long Scandinavian past. Although now part of Scotland, until the second half of the fifteenth century both sets of islands owed allegiance to the king of Norway, and Norn rather than Lowland Scots was still the main spoken language.

In the Shetland Islands there was a belief that way out at sea lived a serpent that took six hours to draw in its breath and another six to let it out. This explained why there were high tides and low tides, twice each day!

Retold by George Douglas (ed.), *Scottish Fairy and Folk Tales*, 1893, and Ernest W. Marwick, *The Folklore of Orkney and Shetland*, 1975.

HOW MUSIC CAME TO THE WORLD

The quetzal is a bird that lives in the remote, cloud-covered rain forests of southern Mexico and Guatemala. The male bird has two extraordinarily long tail feathers that ripple behind him as he flies. With the slightest movement, they shimmer and change color from shades of green through turquoise to blue. *Coatl* means "snake." Thus Quetzalcoatl is a bird-snake. But he is more usually called a feathered snake or plumed serpent. He is primarily a wind god and creator. The supreme god's name is Texcatlipoca, which means "Smoking Mirror."

Quetzalcoatl is the dominant decorative motif in the ancient buildings of the high plateaus of Mexico. Some sculptures depict him as a great swirl of long, reedlike feathers with a snake's head emerging from the top. A human face is sometimes framed within his open jaws, while hands and feet can be glimpsed among the feathers.

Birds' feathers were used by the Aztecs to make superb cloaks and head-dresses. The most valued feathers and featherwork were called "shadows of the Sacred Ones."

This story is based on a poem from a sixteenth-century manuscript, in Nahuatl, the language of the Aztecs and the Toltecs before them. For an English translation, see C. Burland, I. Nicholson, H. Osborne, *Mythology of the Americas*, 1970.

THE ONE AND ONLY MINOTAUR

The story of the Minotaur, though generally termed a Greek myth, probably recalls something of the traditions of the much earlier, great Cretan civilization. The first palace at Knossos was built about 1900 B.C., and for the next five hundred years, as each palace was destroyed by earthquake or fire, another was built on top of the previous one. Archaeologists have discovered bull decorations throughout the last palace—bulls' heads, bulls' horns, and a vivid wall painting depicting the sport of bull jumping, which happened every springtime. Acrobats, both young men and young women, had to seize a charging bull by the horns, turn somersaults over his back, and land on the ground behind. Ancient Egyptian gods and goddesses often had a human body with an animal head, such as a cat, a hawk, or—like the Minotaur—a bull.

THREE FABULOUS EGGS

Nagas can change shape—one moment they can be a hooded snake, the next human, or, as shown in some stone carvings, human from the waist up. Usually they are gentle. But if angered, they are able, with a single glance, to turn a person to ashes. Female Nagas (sometimes called Nagini) are beautiful and may marry humans.

All Nagas love jewels, especially rubies. They live underwater or underground in jewel-studded palaces full of treasures, flowers, singing, and dancing. They are godlike beings and are important in Hindu and Buddhist myths and art throughout much of India, and also in countries farther east such as Java, Cambodia, and, as in this story, Burma.

Retold by Maung Htin Aung, *Burmese Folktales*, 1948.

BIRD OF THE SUN

The Phoenix is the Greek name for the mythical Egyptian bird the *bennu*. Both names mean "palm tree." The only bird of its kind, the Phoenix is a symbol of the sun. It is said to live east of Egypt, in either Arabia or India. Writers disagree about how long the bird lives, but five hundred years is the most common opinion.

See R. Van Den Broek (translated by I. Seeger), *The Myth of the Phoenix*, 1972.